I AM A WOMAN. I AM A TREASURE!

NOTES TO SELF

FOR THE JOURNEY AHEAD

(C)2020 DAMOLA TREASURE OKENLA

ISBN: 978-1-948971-02-7

I0164561

Designed by Damola Treasure Okenla

Published By:

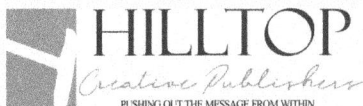

HILLTOP
Creative Publishers
PUSHING OUT THE MESSAGE FROM WITHIN

FROM:

....

TO:

....

I AM A WOMAN. I AM A TREASURE! NOTES TO SELF
For The Journey Ahead

Life may have stolen stuff from you, including your dignity and reputation, but the power for recovery and restoration lies within you. And nobody can take that from you.

There is the power of life and death upon the tongue; that is why you need to talk positively to yourself. Apart from talking to God and listening to Him, you must learn to speak and listen to yourself,

" Your words are so powerful that you will kill or give life."(Proverbs 18:21)

God is not limited by what appears limiting. God can move beyond your limitations to get you to your destination.

Start to #DECLAREIT!

I am awesomely crafted and created for a unique purpose.

I thank you, God, for making me so mysteriously complex!Everything you do is marvelously breathtaking.It simply amazes me to think about it!How thoroughly you know me, Lord!

--Psalm 139:14

God is my STRONG TOWER and my STRENGTH in my weakness. I am strengthened so that I may please Him and live my life before Him in His life-giving light.

The Lord is my revelation-light to guide me along the way; [b]he's the source of my salvation to defend me every day.I fear no one!I'll never turn back and run from you, Lord;surround and protect me.2 When evil ones come to destroy me,they will be the ones who turn back.

__Psalm 27:1

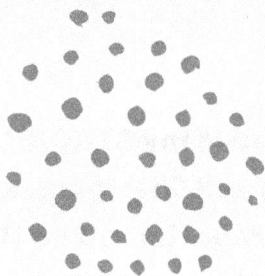

66

Life can only be understood backwards; but it must be lived forwards

SOREN KIERKEGAARD

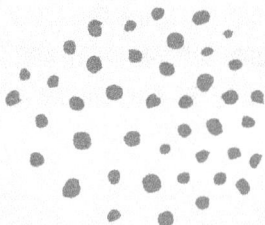

Now I can say to myself: "relax and rest, be confident and serene, for the LORD rewards fully those who simply trust in Him and I have placed all my hope and trust in Him."

"But blessed are those who trust in the Lord   and have made the Lord their hope and confidence.

__ Jeremiah 17:7

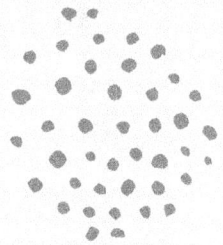

66

The future belongs to those who believe in the beauty of their dreams.

ELEANOR ROOSEVELT

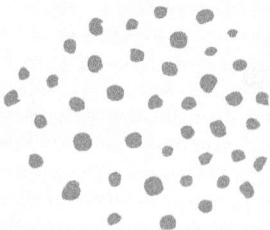

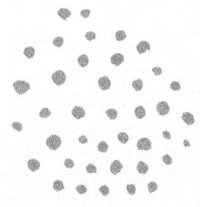

66

Acceptnace
says,True,this is
my situation at the
moment.I'll look
unblinkingly at the
reality of it . But I
will also open my
hands to accept
willingly whatever
a loving Father
sends me.

CATHERINE MARSHALL

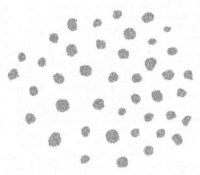

I'm not useless but worthy, and I have something valuable to contribute to the society, regardless of my past mistakes .

For the lovers of God may suffer adversityand stumble seven times,but they will continue to rise over and over again.

 __Proverbs 24:16

I love and admire other women without forgetting my unique style and walking in it. I have learned to live in my own style.

Let everyone be devoted to fulfill the work God has given them to do with excellence, and their joy will be in doing what's right and being themselves, and not in being affirmed by others.
__Galatians 6:4

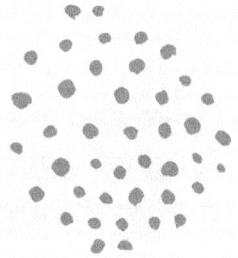

> **"**
> Never be afraid to trust an unknown future to an unknown God.

CORRIE TEN BOOM

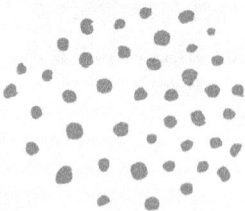

I am on the journey of discovery- my authentic self and what I am capable of doing. I am going to own it and walk in it.

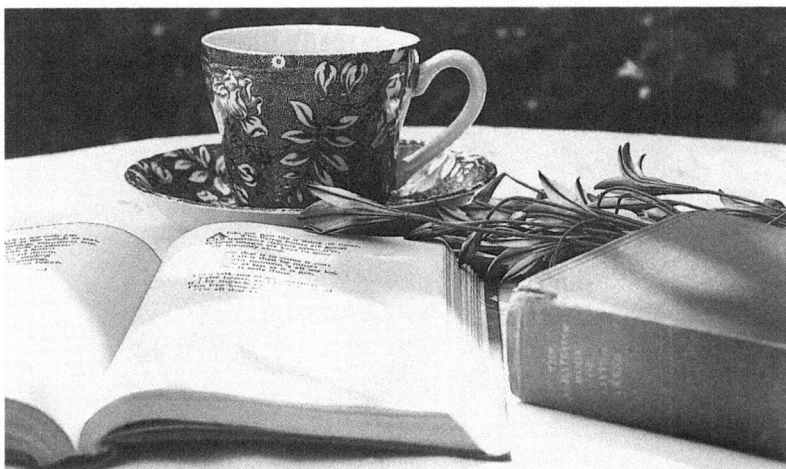

We have become his poetry, a re-created people that will fulfill the destiny he has given each of us, for we are joined to Jesus, the Anointed One. Even before we were born, God planned in advance our destiny and the good works[b] we would do to fulfill it!
_ Ephesians 2:10

I have my unique style, original and not a copy of anyone. I know who God says I am; no identity crisis or confusion.

But when He, Who had chosen and set me apart [even] before I was born and had called me by His grace (His undeserved favor and blessing), saw fit and was pleased.
__ Galatians 1:15

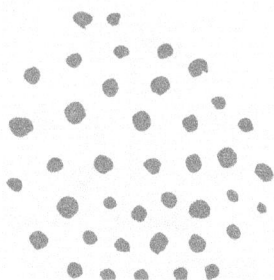

66

In order to be irreplaceable one always be different.

COCO CHANEL

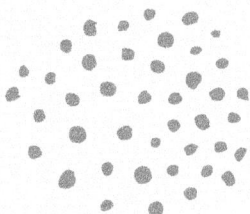

I don't deny the fact that my life had been messy, but the truth is that my ugly past cannot keep me from my glorious future.

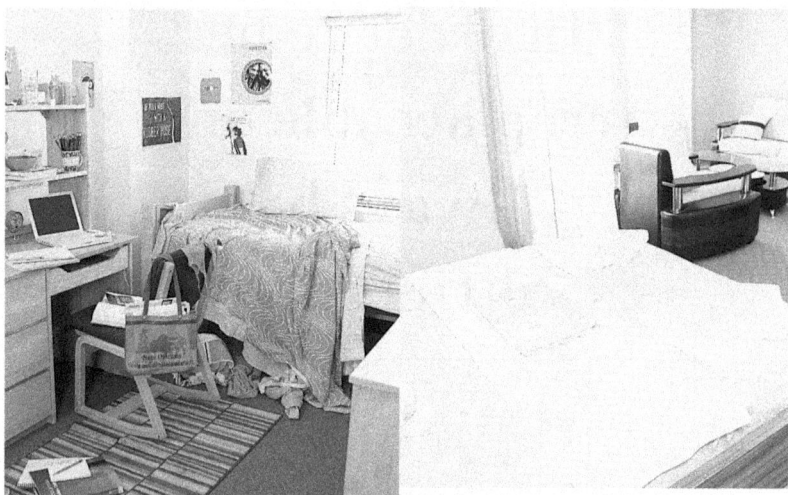

But the Lord says,"Do not cling to events of the past   or dwell on what happened long ago. Watch for the new thing I am going to do.   It is happening already—you can see it now!I will make a road through the wilderness   and give you streams of water there.

__ Isaiah 43:18 -19

I have the confidence to go after what is rightfully mine. I shall indeed pursue, overtake, and recover all!

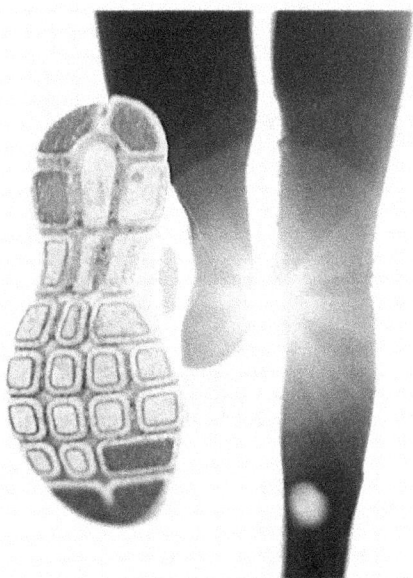

And David inquired of the Lord, saying, Shall I pursue this troop? Shall I overtake them? The Lord answered him, Pursue, for you shall surely overtake them and without fail recover all.

__1 Samuel 30:8

17

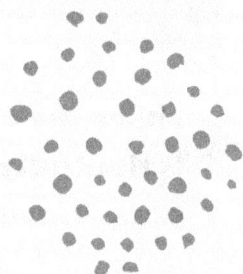

66

The most incredible
beauty and the
most satisfying
way of life come
from affirming
your own
uniqueness.

JANE FONDA

18

I am gracefully endowed to pursue much more than the life of a victim, divorcee, lonely single, or any label at all. I refuse to play the victim; I reject the victim mentality.

Yet amid all these things we are more than conquerors [a]and gain a surpassing victory through Him Who loved us.

__ Romans 8:37

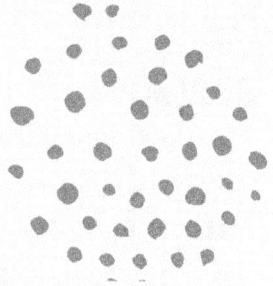

"

Always be a first-
rate version of
yourself, instead of
a second-rate
version of
somebody else.

JUDY GARLAND

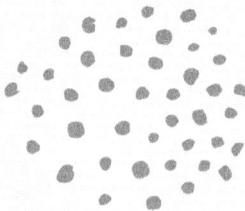

Neither my predicament or my blunders have the power to stop me; I'm getting up and moving forward because destiny is waiting for me.

Weapons made to attack you   won't be successful:words spoken against you   won't hurt at all.

__ Isaiah 54:17

I'm wired to impact my generation. My ugly past does not render me useless, but empowered and equipped me for the future, not just for me, but for many yet unborn.

"Now when David had served God's purpose in his own generation, he fell asleep; he was buried with his ancestors and his body decayed.

__Acts 13:36

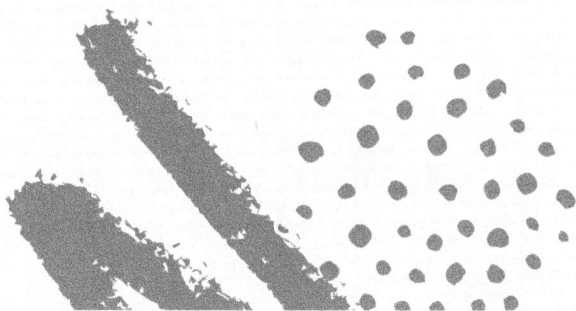

66

I have never felt
more confident in
myself, more clear
on who I am as a
woman.

MICHELLE OBAMA

Honestly, I have had bad experiences. I have gone through rough times. I may have been mistreated, but one thing is sure; putting all together, something beautiful is happening out of it all.

So we are convinced that every detail of our lives is continually woven together to fit into God's perfect plan of bringing good into our lives, for we are his lovers who have been called to fulfill his designed purpose.

__Romans 8:28

24

What anyone thinks about me, don't matter anymore. All things, I say, all things are working out for my good. All of the disappointment, rejection, failure, mistakes, and the shame I went through are working together to bring beauty out of the ashes.

So we are convinced that every detail of our lives is continually woven together to fit into God's perfect plan of bringing good into our lives, for we are his lovers who have been called to fulfill his designed purpose.

__Romans 8:28

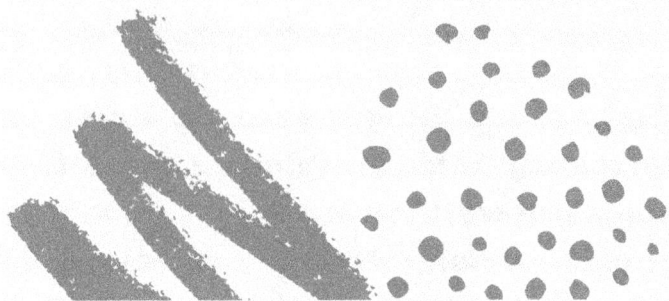

"

Hope is favorable
and confident
expectation; it's an
expectant attitude
that something
good is going to
happen and things
will work out, no
matter what
situation we are
facing

JOYCE MEYER

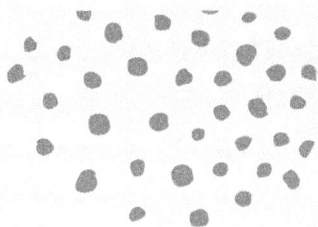

26

I don't have a choice but to be bold and brave to pursue my purpose. My destiny and the destinies of many are at stake.

I've commanded you to be strong and brave. Don't ever be afraid or discouraged! I am the Lord your God, and I will be there to help you wherever you go.

_JOSHUA 1:9

My story may not be the one to boast about, but I'm not going to allow anyone, no matter who, to ridicule me.

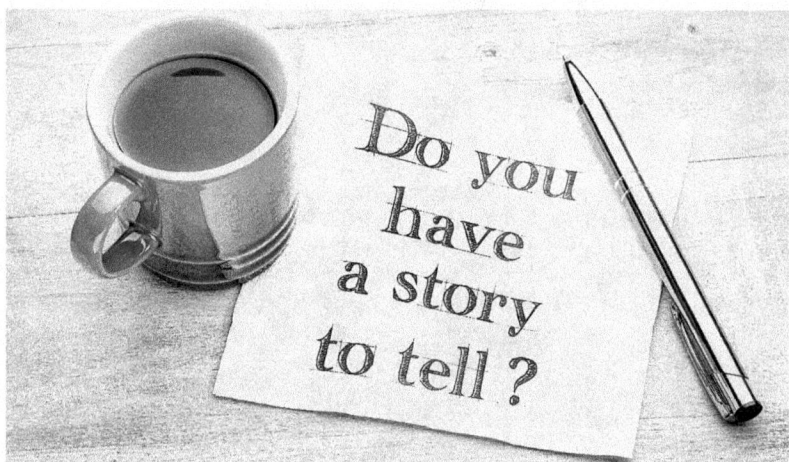

So now the case is closed. There remains no accusing voice of condemnation against those who are joined in life-union with Jesus, the Anointed One.

__ Romans 8:1

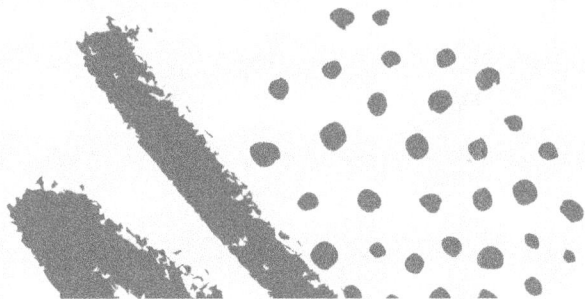

66

Character cannot
be developed in
ease and quiet.
Only through
experience of trial
and suffering can
the soul be
strengthened,
ambition inspired,
and success
achieved ,

HELEN KELLER

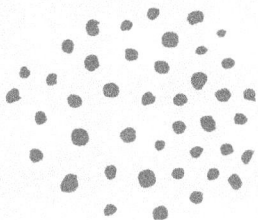

29

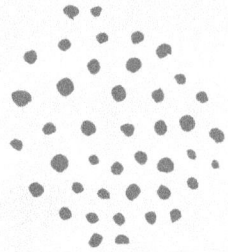

66

You cannot stay
where you are and
go with God. You
cannot continue
doings your way
and accomplish
God's purposes in
His ways. Your
thinking cannot
come close to God's
thoughts. For you
to do the will of
God, you must
adjust your life to
Him, His purposes,
and His ways.

HENRY BLACKBABY

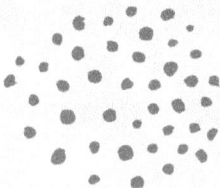

30

I am on the journey of fulfillment of destiny; I understand that I have to invest in my future, and I'm not playing around.

" I am your Creator,   and before you were born, I chose you to speak for me   to the nations."
++Jeremiah 1:5

My source of ridicule is turning to a stepping ladder of a miracle. I am expecting a significant restoration.

Instead of shame and dishonor,   you will enjoy a double share of honor.You will possess a double portion of prosperity in your land,   and everlasting joy will be yours.

__Isaiah 61:7

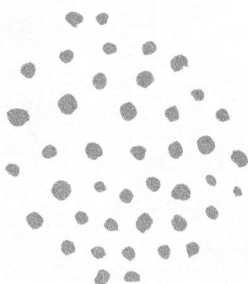

"

Isn't it nice to think that tomorrow is a new day with no mistakes in it yet?

L,M, MONTGPMERY

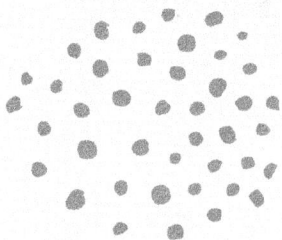

My creator purposely endows me with skills and gifts for the benefits of humanity, and I'm no longer holding back.

"Look, I have specifically chosen Bezalel son of Uri, grandson of Hur, of the tribe of Judah. I have filled him with the Spirit of God, giving him great wisdom, ability, and expertise in all kinds of crafts.He is a master craftsman, expert in working with gold, silver, and bronze. He is skilled in engraving and mounting gemstones and in carving wood. He is a master at every craft!

__Exodus 31:3-5

I will not allow my feelings or other people's opinions of me to stand in the way of my progress.

For the Spirit that God has given us does not make us timid; instead, his Spirit fills us with power, love, and self-control.

2 Timothy 1:7

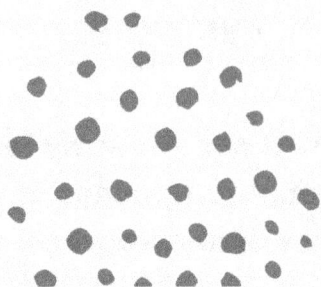

"

The beginning is always today.

MARY SHELLEY

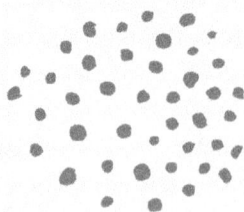

My pursuit and my strategy to fulfill my destiny may not be conventional or appealing, but that is how God wants me to do it, and I'm committed to doing it that way.

I cry out to God Most High,[a]   to God who will fulfill his purpose for me.
__ Psalm 57:2

I am willing and ready to commit, and invest in my destiny, popular or unpopular, appreciated or unappreciated, encouraged or discouraged, misunderstood, or understood; I'm soaring!

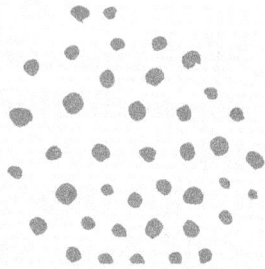

66

The man who
leaves you is
simply
clearing the
way for the
one you
deserve.

NAIDE P. OBIANG

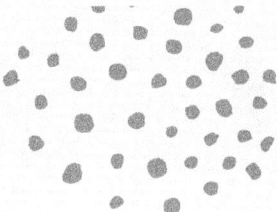

Sometimes I find myself between a rock and a hard place; I will not allow fear to take over me. For God did not give me a spirit of timidity -of cowardice, of craven and cringing and fawning fear, but He has given me a spirit of POWER and LOVE and CALM and WELL-BALANCED mind and DISCIPLINE and SELF-CONTROL.

No matter the situation confronting me to stop me, I'm not giving in. I have the boldness and the confidence to go out, to correct my errors, and walk-in my God's ordained destiny.

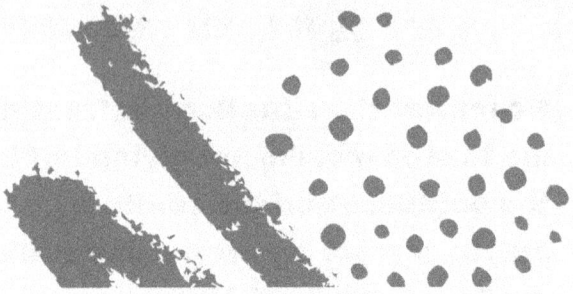

66

Some beautiful paths can't be discovered without getting lost.

EROL OZAN

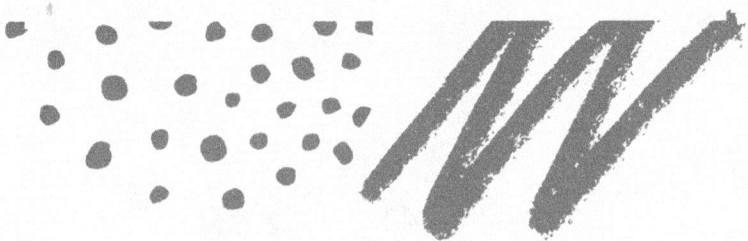

I'm armed with the faith and not fear to step out to become all that God has ordained me to be and not confined by my unfortunate circumstances.

Jesus said to him, "What do you mean 'if'? If you are able to believe, all things are possible to the believer."

__Marks 9:23

I AM A WOMAN. I AM A TREASURE!

I refuse to allow my failure to entrap me. I see it as an opportunity to attempt something new as demonstrations, lectures, speeches, mentoring, coaching, and more.

My fellow believers, when it seems as though you are facing nothing but difficulties see it as an invaluable opportunity to experience the greatest joy that you can! For you know that when your faith is tested[a] it stirs up power within you to endure all things. And then as your endurance grows even stronger it will release perfection into every part of your being until there is nothing missing and nothing lacking

.

__James 1: 2-4

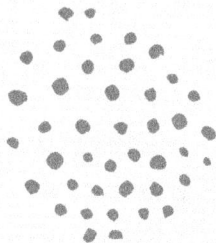

66

Yes I'm
seeking for
someone to
help me, so
that someday
I will be the
someone to
help some
other than
me.

VIGNESH KARTHI

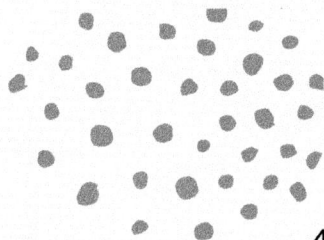

I AM A WOMAN. I AM A TREASURE!

I work with other women- helping, and motivating them to rise and occupy their positions in destiny, rather than pulling them down.

Be free from pride-filled opinions, for they will only harm your cherished unity. Don't allow self-promotion to hide in your hearts, but in authentic humility put others first and view others as more important than yourselves.

__ Phillipians 2:3

My ugly circumstances may make me think it's over, but I have this unshakable confidence to continue to make a move towards my destiny. Bottom line-- I'm not giving up!

And he also says,"My righteous ones will live from my faith.[b]   But if fear holds them back,   my soul is not content with them!

__Hebrews 10:38

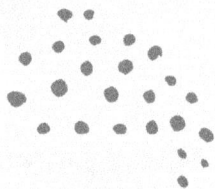

> **"**
> Faith in
> small things
> has a
> repercussion
> s that ripple
> all the way
> out . In a
> huge, dark
> room, a little
> match can
> light up the
> place.

JONI EARECKSON TADA

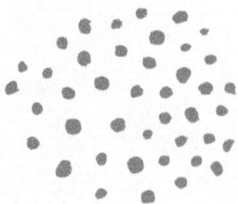

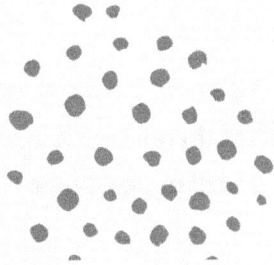

66

One can never consent to creep when one feels an impulse to soar.

HELEN KELLER

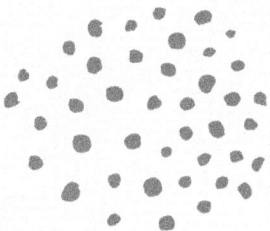

I cannot allow anyone or anything to hold me back anymore, not my age, gender, or race.

And don't be intimidated by those who are older than you; simply be the example they need to see by being faithful and true in all that you do. Speak the truth[a] and live a life of purity and authentic love as you remain strong in your faith.
__ 1 Timothy 4:12

It's time to free my mind off negative thoughts and fill it with productive and progressive ideas that births hope and satisfaction.

So keep your thoughts continually fixed on all that is authentic and real, honorable and admirable, beautiful and respectful, pure and holy, merciful and kind. And fasten your thoughts on every glorious work of God,praising him always.

__Philippians 4:8

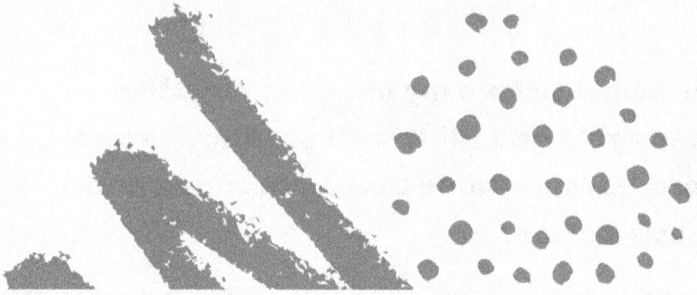

> **"**
> Compare
> youself only
> to who you
> were
> yesteday. Be
> Your own
> competition

———————

ANONNYMOUS

My future depends solely on God's plans and purposes for me and not on the opinions of men.

I alone know the plans I have for you, plans to bring you prosperity and not disaster, plans to bring about the future you hope for.

__ Jeremiah 29:11

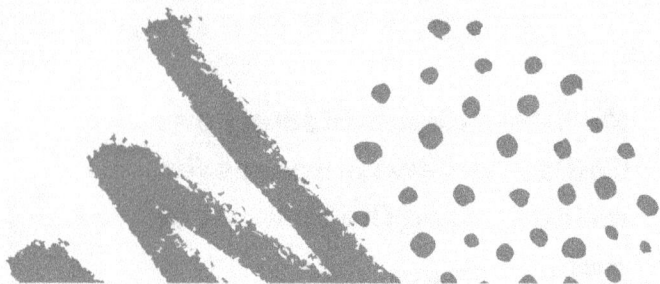

"

I raise up my
voice -not so
that I can
shout, but so
that those
without
voice can be
heard.

MALALA YOUSAFAI

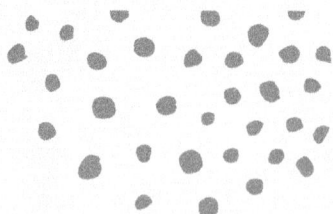

"

If you want
something
said, ask a
man; if you
want
something
done, ask a
woman.

MARGARET THATCHER

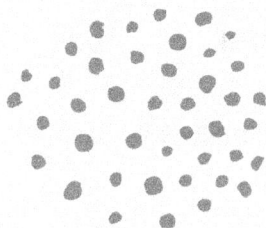

PUBLISHED BOOKS BY DAMOLA

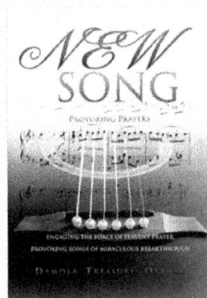

BOOKS AVAILABLE ON AMAZON

https://www.damolatreasureokenla.com/books-by-damola/

WHO AM I?

I am Damola Treasure Okenla (DTO). I am on a mission to help women to unwrap their hidden potentials buried under traumas and trials; repurposing their pain to profit having done the same.

MORE ABOUT DAMOLA

As an award-winning author of several Christian books and a highly sought-after inspirational speaker, Damola Treasure Okenla is dedicated to uplifting others mentally, spiritually and emotionally. For more than ten years, she has partnered with individuals and groups to inspire and motivate others to live the life God intended for them to live—assisting them in rebuilding and recovering from losses and setbacks in life. As the president and founder of Life Encounters, Inc., a non-profit organization that is dedicated to self-discovery and recovery.

 Damola facilitates seminars, workshops and retreats to usher others into purpose fulfillment. Her organization, like her books, is a small reflection of her passion and mission for the advocacy of spiritual freedom and empowerment. Damola serves as the president and founder of Hilltop Publishing, where she assists Christian authors with publishing and social media management for their book projects—positioning them for excellence in the marketplace.

Apart from ministry, Damola works as an accountant and project manager, and holds a Master's in Public Administration. More than anything, Damola is on a mission to help others discover their true potential, live a life of purpose, and earn a profit while doing it.For more information or bookings,
visit www.damolatreasureokenla.com or call 800.767.0728.

STAY CONNECTED

@IAMATREASUREDWOMAN

@TREASUREDWOMAN

@IAMATREASUREDWOMAN

WWW.IAMATREASUREDWOMAN.COM

www.ingramcontent.com/pod-product-compliance
Lightning Source LLC
Chambersburg PA
CBHW060538030426
42337CB00021B/4324